I0437325

Notes to Myself on

GOOD THINGS TO REMEMBER

By Leland Davis

Author of LIFE IS FOR LOVING IT!

authorHOUSE™

1663 LIBERTY DRIVE, SUITE 200
BLOOMINGTON, INDIANA 47403
(800) 839-8640
WWW.AUTHORHOUSE.COM

First published by AuthorHouse 09/16/05

ISBN: 1-4208-8751-3 (e)
ISBN: 1-4208-6390-8 (sc)

Library of Congress Control Number: 2005905236

Printed in the United States of America
Bloomington, Indiana

This book is printed on acid-free paper.

For Patsy

Always and Forever
The Light of My Life

Foreword

How many times over the years I have reached for a scrap of paper or underlined a passage in a book or quotation, to note something that seemed both wise and useful. However, when I review my notes I recall frequently some of these guidelines that I have simply let drift from my memory and have neglected to practice.

As C. S. Lewis once cautioned:

"Often we need not so much to be taught as to be reminded."

It is surprising to me, and a little dismaying, to realize that I have failed to practice something that I had earlier discovered to be so true and beneficial.

What is the remedy? It is obvious: a brief and regular review, perhaps taking only a few minutes, of things worth remembering. And that is the purpose of this book: to summarize, briefly enough for quick and regular review, words of wisdom I have found to be important enough to remember.

The pen is mightier than the sword. Its power to vanquish falsehood and injustice is legendary.

Indeed, it is not only a weapon but is unchallenged as an instrument for proclaiming beauty, tenderness, mercy, wisdom and love.

Clarence Day must have felt this same sense of reverence when he wrote: "The world of books is the most remarkable creation of man. Nothing else that he builds ever lasts. Monuments fall. Nations perish. Civilizations grow old and die out and after an era of darkness new races build others. But in the world of books are volumes that have seen this happen again and again, still young, still fresh as the day they were written, still telling men's hearts of the hearts of men centuries dead."

Beware the broad brush.

"All men are chauvinists." "Women are poor drivers." "Psychiatry is hokum." "The Irish are hot-tempered."

We hear, too often, sweeping statements that betray not only prejudice and ignorance but the human desire to simplify, to categorize. Intelligent, well-informed opinion takes more forbearance than sometimes we're willing to put forth.

Snap judgments are easy, yet frequently wrong. ("He's a jerk!" "She's an air head!") We need to hesitate and reflect before forming an opinion expressed in a moment of pique or irritation. We base our attitudes too often on details or incidents that later turn out to be far from accurate.

Laziness is sometimes at the core of our unwillingness to really understand a situation or to fully *know* a person and why he or she acts or feels a certain way. Someone once said, "If we knew the secret history of our enemies we would discover enough sorrow and suffering to disarm all hostility."

Isn't it always best to reject an unfavorable judgment based on momentary or superficial impressions? One of life's most precious blessings is friendship with different kinds of people. We need to fight against the tendency to write off those we meet for the first or second time who "rubs us the wrong way." Yet these same folk may later turn out to be good friends. There is much wisdom in the old French proverb: "Most men improve on acquaintance."

Every day a bonus.

Whether you are eight or eighteen or eighty or somewhere in between, when you open your eyes in the morning thank God for another day. Never take it for granted that you are here and alive. There were no guarantees yesterday that you would be here today and there are none for tomorrow. Decide to relish the coming 24 hours as a bonus and let your first waking words be, "This is the day which the Lord hath made. I will be glad and rejoice in it!"

"Your head creates your world."

I can't remember where I read that, but nothing comes closer to affecting your outlook on life than your thoughts. It's been said so many different ways ("I think, therefore I am." "As a man thinketh in his heart so is he." etc.) But I am particularly fond of the idea that your thoughts actually *create* your world. Someone has called it "the law of magnetic attraction." In other words, you actually draw to yourself either happiness or unhappiness by the kind of thoughts you *allow* yourself to think. The trick here is to set up a kind of internal alarm system that keeps you aware of the intrusion of unwanted thoughts and alerts you to shift them immediately into positive channels. That way you can count on actually creating your own reality.

Attitude is everything.

The effect our attitudes have on our lives is simply overwhelming. With a healthy attitude we address both opportunities and setbacks with optimism, cheerfulness and determination to do the best we can. Success in any endeavor rarely follows a negative attitude. Jim Rohn, one of the great motivational speakers, has said that if two people swim a river, one carrying lead and the other cork, the challenge is hardly the same for both. A healthy attitude is the cork you carry in your swim through life; a negative attitude is lead.

Well, what do you want? Really want?

I have found that asking myself this question when making decisions produces surprisingly good results and helps prevent making poor choices. Ask it concerning something as trivial as choosing a book to read or as life-affecting as choosing a wife. In between are a whole world of decisions, short and long-range, that can affect our sense of well-being and happiness throughout life.

The happiest of all.

There is a legend about a little lady who was always the happiest person in the small village where she lived. Urged to tell why she was so happy she would say only that when she was a little girl a fairy told her the secret. But she would never tell what it was. Finally, when she was very old, the villagers feared she would die without revealing her secret, and so they asked her once again what it was. She replied, "The fairy told me that everyone needs love, more than anything, and if I was always loving I would always be giving people what they need the most. And that would make me very happy. And so it has been all my life."

"The essential invisible. Look for it in everyone you meet."

This is a quote from Mr. Rogers, the gentle, loving host for the long-running children's TV program, Mr. Roger's Playhouse. What is this "essential invisible?" It is the core of our personality, shaped by our physical and emotional makeup and by every experience we have had since birth. Our relationships are greatly improved with each other when we are aware of it and are sensitive to clues to its nature.

Define your terms.

It is surprising how often we find ourselves in the middle of an argument when neither side has defined the terms he is using. Take the word "success." I may define success in the context of material wealth while my neighbor regards "success" in terms of a lifestyle devoted to serving others. Clarity is always enhanced when each side asks the other to "define your terms."

Not perfect, but OK.

Sometimes we ask so much – too much – of ourselves. "Whatever is worth doing is worth doing well." We've all heard that since childhood. Many of us grew up expected to do everything perfectly, and to feel less worthy if we don't. But according to psychologist Wayne Dyer, there's nothing wrong with an ordinary bicycle ride, or a so-so painting, or a mediocre golf game so long as we enjoy what we do. Yes, perfection must be sought in some things (brain surgery for example). But the idea that everything we do should be done perfectly robs us of so much pleasure. If something you enjoy doing isn't done perfectly, well, that's perfectly OK.

Why?

A wise man once said, "There's magic in a question mark. 'Why' leads children and geniuses to achievement." Getting to the core of the matter by asking "Why?" and other pertinent questions can indeed put us on the road to knowledge and, even more important, to understanding. We should never hesitate to ask for more information when we want to know something. Every great discovery came about because someone started out by asking "Why?" Newton, asking why the apple dropped to earth, led eventually to man's walking on the moon.

Self talk.

When faced with some unpleasantness, choose a word or two to speak silently to yourself when you are tempted to respond in a way you might regret later. How about the question "later" itself? Saying "later" prompts you to reflect briefly on how you will feel after the incident has passed, depending on the response you make now. It is a practice that can help you avoid feeling somewhat diminished if you react too quickly, especially if emotion is involved.

Don't expect never to be rejected.

It's incredible how many of us expect always to be liked, by everybody. Life doesn't work that way. No matter how attractive you may feel or how hard you try to please, sometimes you'll be liked and sometime you won't. It's best just to accept this as a fact of life and move out openly embracing every opportunity to participate in society without expecting 100% approval all the time.

My Dad.

How can I ever describe adequately what he meant to me: his sensitivity and compassion, his wisdom and insight, his disdain for hypocrisy – all the complex facets of his personality. I can only try.

His influence on me is still profound. The Bible he sent me when I was overseas in World War II sits on my desk today, his favorite passages underlined with his personal notes in the margins. The pages are tattered from my own underlining and almost daily reading. He had written inside the front cover: "All the ore isn't gold, but all the gold comes from the ore." This phrase has guided me all through the years in my search for understanding and guidance from this blessed book. Somehow the truth seems to shine through when I realize that the "gold" really is there but that some things in the Bible are puzzling and unclear. "Take what works for you, son, and don't trouble yourself about the rest," he wrote. "Wisdom is justified by all her children" was one of his favorite quotations.

My earliest memories are of my Dad kneeling and praying with me at bedtime, then tucking me in and kissing me good night. The sense of security I felt, the feeling of being loved and protected by this wonderful man, was blissful.

Why am I recalling all this now? Simply to remind myself once again of the priceless spiritual foundation that resulted from his loving wisdom and nurture in my youth. I hope I have been at least half as successful with my own children.

Well being. Isn't that what we're after?

Stay cool. Balance emotion with motion. Keep busy. Will Durant writes, "To be busy is the secret of grace, and half the secret of content. Let us ask the gods not for possessions but for things to do."

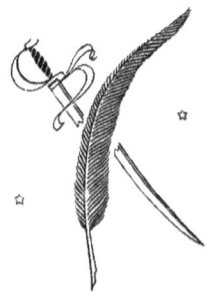

Who knows how much more time he has?

This morning, as perfect as any morning I have ever seen (I am 76 as I write this), I walked through the grounds of St. Mary's Seminary. The sky was flawless, a solid curtain of the bluest blue possible, the air cool on my face, the sun dappling the leaves, newly green in their springtime youth – a day I can only describe as an "oh my!" day. For sheer, stately loveliness, no structure, in my opinion, can match St. Mary's. There is a specialness about it, and I always pause on these walks of mine to wonder at its beauty. The combination of the day and view touches my soul.

So why should my thoughts turn to how much time I have left to relish such moments? I suppose it is the urgency with which I want to drink it all in, all of it, because I know that such moments are indeed growing fewer and being aware of this, I want to gobble them up with the fervor of a starving man presented with a luscious meal. My feelings are not prompted by uneasiness about my advancing age or about what lies "out there." I just want to be fully aware now of how beautiful this day is, and I am.

Lists, oh Lord, those lists.

They are supposed to help get organized, set priorities, lead to accomplishing "things to do" each day. As helpful as I find them to be, overall, I sometimes hate the thought of those darn lists, for they put binds on me and make me feel constricted, tight, unfree. They set a structure for my days when I don't want to feel structured. I want to feel free, to fly, to do what I darn well please.

And yet, I realize that without some kind of plan for addressing those tasks I know are the "important" ones, they don't get done, and another day passes with that empty, frazzled feeling. Maybe I just make them too long, trying to get everything down that it would be ideal to get done. Maybe limit them to the most important, the most pressing. But, I am just not going to victimize myself any more with those darn, overlong lists.

Upset? Do something. *Anything!*

Nothing settles me down more quickly when I'm frustrated or when I have lost my cool than to get physically active, even if it is nothing more that to take a walk, wash the car, clean out a closet – whatever is at hand. Being in motion works like a tranquilizer and doesn't take long. What *doesn't* work is to sit and stew about what has upset me. That only makes it worse and surely takes longer to work out than simply to *get busy*, and to get busy quickly. It works.

Companionship with Jesus.

What a gift, to be able to conceive of Jesus walking beside you, all the time. It is a gift He gave to all of us when He said, "... and lo, I am with you alway, even unto the end of the world." To accept such a promise, and make His calm and loving presence the centerpiece of your life, think of how that would alter your every behavior, your every word, your every thought. What a change such a companionship would make in the life of someone drifting through life, a victim of negative moods, unable to relate healthfully to his neighbors, his co-workers and himself. What a difference!

And yet that companion stands ready to accompany us whenever we ask Him to. That's all we have to do. "Go with me Jesus from now on and forever."

10 years from now.

One of the most valuable of all the wise suggestions my father passed along to me (and there were so many) was to ask myself often, "10 years from now, what will you wish you had done today?" How many times I have asked myself that question, and how often my answer has guided me in making decisions, especially with regard to the family. For example, when the kids were young, and I had a choice to spend some extra time with them or go another way, answering that question gave me the answer, and now, with them grown and gone from home, it gives me much peace to remember how often I chose the kids. Same thing with my darling Patsy. I know that if she goes first, the terrible loss I will feel will be softened some by the memories of uncountable times when I chose to be with her rather than do something else.

Here and now.

Someone has called it "the precious present," those special moments when we suddenly realize just how precious they are: an unexpected warm feeling for a loved one, or coming upon a flaring sunset that stops us in our tracks, or our first glimpse of a sparkling dawn, fresh and new ... moments like those. Recognizing and cherishing those special moments when they happen, *here and now,* is what happiness is all about. There are many more of them than we may realize. The trick is to stay alert and recognize them when they occur. They are part of the true pleasure of living, the part that endures in our memory.

The Arab kid.

I have many poignant memories of World War II but possibly the saddest is that of a ragged little Arab kid digging barehanded into a garbage can outside our mess tent in North Africa. We were on our way to a base in Italy from which we would fly bombing missions over Europe, and had landed to refuel.

It was the first time I had ever witnessed the kind of hunger that would cause someone to transfer a glob of fly-specked slop directly into his mouth.

What kind of poverty, what kind of desperation would make someone do such a thing? The utter hopelessness of the whole scene depressed me for days.

What kind of future would this kid have? What kind of health awaited him as he grew, deprived of the nourishment the body needs to ward off disease? What would happen to him?

Something happened to me at that moment. I made two commitments, one, never again, ever, to complain about a meal, and two, to be thankful, always, for whatever was set before me at mealtime. That was over 60 years ago, but ever since that day, I have bowed my head before eating and thanked God for the food before me. Every meal, ever since.

Know yourself.

"You can have it all ... win the Marathon, write a best seller, paint a masterpiece, become a millionaire. In fact, you can do, be and have anything you really want," so say some pop-psych motivators today.

Looking honestly at ourselves, with total objectivity, we can see that for the most part we have the capacity to be, do and have more. Can we have anything we want?

The truth is, sadly enough, that burn-out, low self-esteem and depression can result from buying into this "no limits" philosophy. Too often people attempt to stretch themselves beyond their natural capacities and end up feeling like failures, unless they succeed in getting what is in reality, beyond them.

The trick is, after giving maximum and sustained effort to achieve certain goals, and failing, we refocus on achievements that are within our capabilities and adjust, cheerfully, to the new reality.

For years, I pushed myself into exhaustion, expecting results that required more energy than I possessed. I finally realized that where energy was concerned, I was a 10 gallon jug, not a 12 gallon jug. When I accepted that fact and adjusted my goals accordingly, I became a happier person.

Know yourself. That's the important thing.

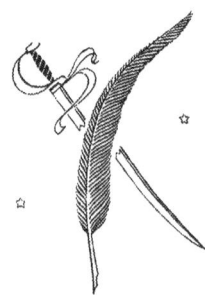

"The art of being wise is the art of knowing what to overlook."

This piece of wisdom from William James, America's foremost psychologist, is a priceless tool for teaching us how to get along with others and to have friends. Our relationships offer frequent opportunities to misunderstand, to take offense, to read into someone's comment something that displeases us. However, rare is the occasion when our negative response will help. Best to follow Mr. James' advice and, most often, "let it pass."

Say something.

Somehow or other I always feel a nice little sense of warmth whenever someone makes a friendly comment to me, especially if they are the first to speak. I suppose it is human nature to want some kind of recognition, some kind of affirmation.

Albert Schweitzer said, "We are all so much together, yet we are all dying of loneliness." Maybe it is that gesture from another person that for the moment reminds us, perhaps even subconsciously, that we exist, that we are somebody, somebody worth speaking to, that we are not alone. For over 50 years I've watched my wife work a special kind of magic by her warm way of affirming people with her spontaneous smile and greeting. How welcome it is to people who may be (who knows?) a little lonely. What a nice little gift we can give to others, simply by being the first to speak, to show a friendly smile.

Know what you don't know.

The wisest among us know what they don't know. I once knew a man with little formal education who was always aware of his lack of understanding of the complexity of successful investing. However, he made it a primary, long-term objective to cultivate the acquaintance of men with proven success in the stock market, and to undertake an in-depth study of respected literature on the subject. As a result he was able to create an income-producing portfolio which enabled him to live very well without the need of a job.

The point is obvious, and, of course, can be applied by any of us who may desire to know something but with little knowledge about how to go about getting it. Seek help from those who know.

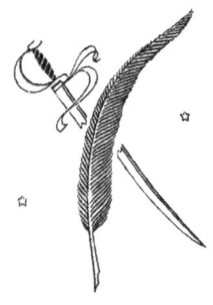

The energy of joy.

I read something somewhere once about "the energy of joy." The phrase strikes me as particularly intriguing – the idea that being joyful really does produce energy, sometimes in abundance. Look at what happens when suddenly you come upon some opportunity to do something you love. What happens? Right then, you feel uplifted, regenerated, leaving behind all thoughts and feelings of tiredness, ready to get going, ready to pursue whatever it was that sparked your interest. Knowing this to be true is a real incentive to be involved as much as possible doing things that give you joy. As Joseph Campbell said, "Follow your bliss."

"The kingdom of God is within you."

He is not "out there" somewhere but His spirit is within your very being, perpetually there to help you do any good thing, to strengthen you in any good task, and to comfort you in any tribulation. You don't have to look for Him anywhere. He is right there within your heart, at all times, wherever you are.

Love, always, in all ways.

Look for ways to extend love to all people you come in contact with. Look at them as God sees them, as His beloved children, just as you look at your own children, with compassion and understanding. We all need love as much as we need to breathe.

In praise of little bits.

In thinking about the subject of personal goals and making the plans to achieve them, I have been struck by the vast potential of small bits of time consistently applied. For the last six months or so on my morning walks, I pass by an old, vacant, dilapidated house in process of being remodeled. Only one person seems to be doing the work, with very little time to devote to it because I can see only small improvements each time I pass by. Gradually, however, a more attractive appearance is taking shape and I feel certain that one day the place will be completed and much beautified.

 It is a classic example of what can be accomplished by using odd moments focused on specific projects. Often when we think of something we would like to complete we are daunted by the thought of the amount of time it would take, time that " we can't or just don't want to take right now." Yet when we apply the "little bits" idea and apply a little math, we find that just 15 minutes a day adds up to over 90 hours a year. (15 x 365 = 5,475 minutes a year, divided by 60) = 90 hours – over 11, 8-hour days!

Imagine all the things you could do with 90 hours! When I think about it, I get goose bumps. Different people would make different lists, of course, but in my own case I can imagine reading many of the great books I haven't read, or getting a good start on learning a foreign language, or becoming much more adept at mediation or memorizing poetry that has moved me, or listening to recordings of great operas (about which I know very little) or take a correspondence course in computers ... the list is practically endless of things I could do with 90 concentrated hours, things that when accomplished would give me pleasure and fulfillment.

As Dr. Seuss might say, "Oh, the things I could do!"

Too much good around to dwell on anything else.

Praise for positive thinking has been stated countless ways, its power to change our moods, our lives even, and has been proven priceless over and over again for centuries. But one aspect hasn't been addressed nearly enough, and that is how to *maintain* a desirable frame of mind when exposure to negatives abounds in the world. One answer that I have found effective is the instant banishment of negative thoughts concerning things I can do nothing about and their replacement by thoughts that give me pleasure. When you come to think of it, there is so much good in the world we should have no problem focusing on things that can uplift us.

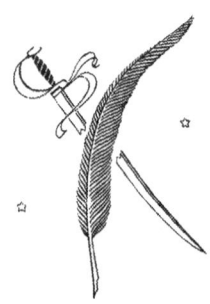

Thank you, God, for green.

I am just so thankful for my eyesight. It is spring, and I try to catch all the colors as I walk in the early morning, the fresh grass ("springing out of the ground with pure shining, after rain") and I am so overwhelmed with thanksgiving that I am wordless. How beautiful. The sky above me is purest blue, the air fresh and even tasty!

Color abounds: delicate, purple violets, red and pink and white roses that seem to speak to me, saying "Hello there, aren't we pretty?"

I even speak to the trees, the sun, the frayed little moon above struggling against the brightening sky. "Hello there, Mr. Sun! Hello Moon!" What poetry! They are my friends, really. "Hello there tree!" I have so many friends on my early walks, and there are no people out yet. Only trees and flowers and sun and air and, well, God, thank you for so much beauty and for my awareness of it. Thank you God, for green and purple and blue and orange and red and ... well, thank you God for this whole wonderful world.

My greatest blessing ...

... is that I am *aware* of my blessings, which have been multiple and precious.

Perhaps what really started this awareness was a line I read somewhere as a youth, which said "Those who simple joys have known are taught to prize them when they are gone." That struck me at the time as a very wise saying, even though I was only twelve or thirteen years old at the time.

For the rest of my life that idea has shaped my attitude, at all times, in all places: blue skies and fresh air in early morning; the taste of the first cup of coffee at breakfast; the lazy sound of locusts in early August; the near-ecstasy of drifting off to sleep after a tiring day. My list of blessings is very long indeed, thanks to my *awareness* of their presence in my life.

Disconnect. You don't have to react.

When the shadow of a disturbing thought comes, like an unwelcome telephone call, why can't I just "hang up" and cut it off from my consciousness? I think I can. I can just refuse to dwell on anything that is negative and turn my attention to more pleasant things. That doesn't mean, of course, that I should deny that certain negatives exist. It does mean, however, that I should give such issues my attention only when I can do something about them.

Switch.

It is very exciting to me to come upon a new way of dealing with any negativity. Just flip the coin of consciousness to whatever is or could be positive in a negative situation. Example: a rather hurtful comment was made recently to my wife by a close relative. When I heard about it, my immediate reaction was one of irritation – even anger – because the comment was uncalled for, even waspish. Before allowing myself to linger on the subject, I deliberately shifted my attention to the desirable traits possessed by the offender. And there were many. This helped soften my feelings and to rethink the context in which the comments were made.

This "cognitive switch" can work in many ways. Sometimes in assessing a personal problem of concern, a deliberate focus on something that is favorable can replace the negative feelings, at least temporarily. This lightens the picture and gives me back some optimism and peace of mind.

You win some, and you lose some.

Ken Keys, in *Handbook of Higher Consciousness*, called this "the basic condition of all life. No one who has ever lived has had enough power to overcome it." But it is so easy to forget. Losing hurts, even though in your heart you know "you can't win 'em all." The main thing is to learn something from every loss, and to look at failure not as something to be ashamed of but simply as information about what didn't work, to be avoided next time you face a similar situation.

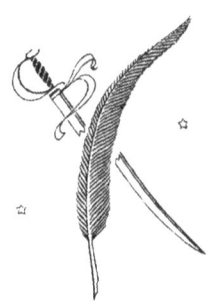

Pray continuously?

The Apostle Paul's injunction was to pray all the time. What do you suppose he was talking about? How could we ever get anything done if all we did was pray? I don't think he meant to do nothing but pray, but to be of such a mind-set that whatever we think about or do is subconsciously God-centered. That way our lives would be shaped automatically by the way God would have us shape them. I think that was what Paul was talking about – "God centeredness" – resulting from a subconscious, therefore constant, prayer of good will and love.

A project, always.

Many years ago I heard Art Linkletter, a radio and TV personality, speak of some activities that make for happy and productive living. One of these, he pointed out, is always to have some kind of project or hobby going, something you look forward to doing that gives you pleasure. It could be anything whatever – stamp collecting, or carving, or learning to play the guitar, or painting, or writing poetry, or gardening – any one of a wide variety of things. The idea is firmly endorsed by mental health professionals everywhere who encourage the pursuit of something pleasurable you can lose yourself in in the doing, that takes you away, that tends to block out everything except that which is at hand. Following Linkletter's suggestion has added much to my enjoyment of life because ever since I heard it, I have had some kind of project under way. I think the idea is essential for good mental health, for a sense of purpose.

You can't force a friendship.

I enjoyed his company. We had met at a seminar and I felt good about our conversation. So several weeks later, I called and asked him to join me for lunch. He responded favorably and we had another fine talk. Several months passed with no communication. I had been stimulated by our exchange of thoughts and ideas so I called him again and suggested another lunch. "Great idea!" So we met again with the same good result. Once more the same scenario took place: no initiation on his part. I did not call him again nor did he call me. About a year later I saw him on the street downtown. After we exchanged greetings I said, "Hey, next time you call. Friendship goes both ways." "Oh yes! Sure thing," he said. I never heard from him again.

Some time later, I shared with my wife a slight sense of hurt over his lack of response. She pointed out something I should have known: friendships don't thrive when obligation is implied. Desire for their maintenance has to be encouraged by both parties.

Friends, I am so grateful for my friends.

They are among my most treasured blessings. I am afraid that in unguarded moments, I drift into a revery about growing older and losing loved ones and facing loneliness (I am 80 as I write this). I don't dwell on these thoughts but when they come, I quickly remind myself of the many people I can call genuine friends. They are like an insurance policy against an isolation that can come too often with the autumn years.

One piece of advice I would offer to anyone at any stage of his or her life is to make a priority to develop friendships. Someone once said, "A friend is a gift you give to yourself." A very precious gift indeed.

Losing your temper? "Beat a wise retreat."

The wise and worldly Jesuit Priest, Balthasar Gracian, centuries ago wrote, "Never act in a passion ... passion drives out reason." How easy it is to lose one's judgment and speak or act negatively under the influence of strong emotion. The result is rarely pleasing to ourselves, and certainly not to others.

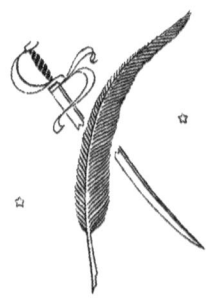

"Always time to add a word, never time to withdraw one."

A guaranteed guide to good relationships. It is so easy to slip and say the first thing that comes to mind when we are agitated, and almost always we would answer differently if we let some time pass before responding. As someone has said, "The best antidote for anger is delay."

Be cautious about first impressions.

Wait for a second, or third, or even fourth contact. Love at first sight has too often led to later, less favorable emotions. Sometimes we are convinced too soon of someone's good or bad qualities. Better to delay before coming to a firm conclusion about anybody, or anything.

"As far as I know."

Pretty good words to use before expressing an opinion about almost any issue. When, indeed, does anyone know everything about anything? A single overlooked fact may change the entire picture. "As far as I know" reminds us of our always incomplete knowledge, keeps us open to new information, and adds a touch of humility lest we appear as a know-it-all.

"I can choose peace, rather than this."

Wise words from Wayne Dyer, psychologist and author. He advises that whenever we find ourselves in the midst of disharmony, if we silently repeat these words, it helps us maintain a calm attitude and be able to judge the issue objectively. What a priceless tool for managing ourselves and to be an oasis of calm in conflict. "I can choose peace rather than this." Use these words as a silent mantra in the midst of any unpleasantness.

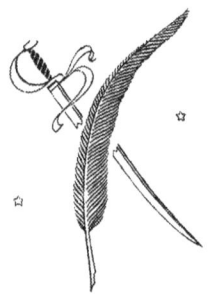

"The way to peace ...

... is to entrust ourselves and all we hold dear to the loving hands of God. He who prays with a perfect trust in the love, wisdom, and power of God will find God's peace."

What a promise. What a way to state it. This is from William Barclay, a clergyman, in a book on the New Testament. I have just participated in a small group discussion on "the nature of God." What is He really like? Is there really a God who is in any way like us in His personal characteristics? Is there any such thing as a "theistic" God, or is He simply the spirit of all that is good and compassionate and beautiful, "the Ground of our Being" as described by John Spong. These were some of the topics discussed which were very disturbing to me, because all my life I have addressed my prayers to a personal God, some "One" who hears me, on a person-to-person basis. How do I pray to "the Ground of our Being.?"

And then. just today, in reviewing some notes I made years ago, I ran across Mr. Barclay's comment, quoted above, and you know what? Suddenly all my turmoil sparked by the discussion seemed to dissolve in the beauty and simplicity of "the way to peace is to entrust ...." That's good enough for me.

Treat yourself as you would treat your very best friend.

We are so hard on ourselves sometimes. It is good to reflect frequently on whether we regard ourselves as tolerantly as we regard someone whose friendship we cherish. We wouldn't expect him or her to be without flaws, perpetually perfect, always doing and saying the right thing, now would we? Then don't expect this kind of perfection from yourself. Try to be the person you would like to be, but learn to accept – and more importantly, to like yourself, because you are the one who is going to have to live with you for the rest of your life.

"I am so sorry."

Someone you know has suffered a sadness or loss. You yearn to offer some assurance of your caring. What can you say? A gentle embrace and a whispered "I am so sorry," will show that you feel their pain and convey your loving concern. More than that, at the moment, may seem intrusive. Better to let it rest with that simple gesture.

"Just do it."

Sincerest thanks to this Nike slogan that seems to be everywhere. What a spur to action! What a kick in the pants! Can you think of a better "first cause" of accomplishment than this little phrase? Looking back, how many satisfactions have you experienced from just "doing it?" Anthony Robbins, prominent writer and motivator, has said that "The greatest gift that extraordinary people have over the average person is their ability to get themselves to take action. It is a gift that any of us can develop within ourselves." That's just what it is too – a gift we can give ourselves. Just do it.

Well, that's always possible.

As I walked into the men's lounge at my golf club there was a discussion going on about a current labor dispute involving our local NFL team, the Bengals. The men were my friends so I sat down and listened. One man was particularly vehement in his condemnation of one side in the dispute. Finally I said, "What's wrong with arbitration? Seems like a pretty good idea." The man who was so upset whirled and said to me, "You don't know what you're talking about!"

I felt surprised and a little angry at such a hostile reply, but something made me smile and say softly, "Well, that's always possible, but ..." and then went on giving some of the reasons supporting my view.

Later, as I reflected on the incident, I was pleased that I handled the situation the way I had. Too often in the past, in similar circumstances, I haven't performed as well. Once in a while I do things right.

The "should" monster.

As I grow older, I keep learning new ways to enjoy life. One way involves how we make the thousands of decisions we make throughout the years. There are three factors involved: there are things we *must* do (die, pay our taxes); there are things we *want* to do (have fun, enjoy our leisure); and there are things we ... what? *should* do.

I have come to see that far too often, the things I "want" to do are shoved aside by the "shoulds." Now, of course, sometimes the shoulds and wants are inseparable, like Siamese twins. If we "want" to have healthy bodies then we "should" eat wisely and exercise. But with only 24 hours in a day, and if we are lucky, 60 or 70 years to live, doesn't it make sense to look hard at all those "shoulds" that divert us from things that we want to enjoy? Maybe we should be more selective about our "shoulds," don't you think?

Out of line.

The other day I noticed the car pulling a little to the left, indicating a slight out of alignment of the front end. It had been so gradual I hardly noticed it.

I little later, I got to thinking about how many times our thinking can be compared to the alignment of an automobile, the way thoughts can slowly, subtly drift into negative channels without our awareness. Unless corrected, like a poorly aligned front end, we're headed toward downer moods, even depression.

The trick here is to be aware, always, of what is going on "upstairs," always, and to keep our thoughts centered on positive things. The key word here is *always*. Our minds have a way of dancing one way and another, thoughts blowing through in a torrent. They need constant monitoring if we want to keep feeling "up," most of the time.

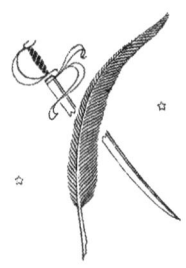

Thank you, God, for problems.

On my "Thank You" walk this morning, while reflecting on all my blessings, it came to me suddenly that I also should be thankful for problems. Sounds odd. Why should anyone be thankful for problems? Problems are nothing but headaches, right? Clouds on the horizon, thorns in the side.

But when I think about a life without any problems, when everything is always hotsy totsy, life flowing along flawlessly, no bumps, then how would I ever be able to appreciate completion, or the satisfaction that comes with a difficulty overcome, or a problem solved? Sounds kind of bland, doesn't it?

Problems build mental muscle, give us the pleasure of competition against adversaries that test us and help us grow. They build our character and increase our knowledge of how to deal with future problems.

Of course, I don't recommend going out of our way looking for problems. But when they come, uninvited though they may be, I should be grateful for the opportunities for growth they can provide.

Long time coming.

What a picture! The portly little ninety year old Picasso, naked to the waist, standing before a giant easel with paint brush in his hand and a bright, excited expression on his face. Picasso, unique in his flare for life and delight in painting, said once, "It takes a very long time to become young." He is obviously someone who has found a youthful joy in life in his autumn years. His comment that it takes "a very long time" should cause us all to reflect seriously as we become older. "Am I learning how to become more excited, energized and joyous – more delighted in life – or are things tending more the other way?"

I think his statement implies, at least it does to me, that to achieve and maintain this youthful *joie d'evivre* takes a long time because it requires not only the maturity that comes with age but also, and even more important, the effort and desire to learn about what if takes "to become young."

Effort and desire, and a constant shifting of our awareness from what is negative to what is beautiful and uplifting and joyous. To do that is indeed "to become young."

Perspective.

I have a small, pocket diary where I keep all my engagements and other data for each day of the current year. This year at the end of December as I started to replace it, something made me stop and casually leaf through the pages. Recalling the crowded weeks and months somehow depressed me. So many commitments, so much busyness and hurry, meetings, travel schedules, dinner and luncheon engagements, reports, assignments – an endless string of activities few of which had added any real value to my life.

It seemed a case of the immediate too often shoving aside the really important. Where was time simply to "loaf and invite my soul?" When had I stopped to listen to music that moved me or to study a sunset? What were the important books I had read which deepened me spiritually? When did I visit an art museum or go to the symphony? How much time had I spent in prayer or meditation?

I picked up my engagement book for the coming year resolved that the next 12 months would see some major changes. Life is too short to allow the immediate to dominate and leave little time for the really important. I'm not going to get that happen again.

Relish!

This morning I took a bike ride. We have had the longest drought I can remember in August and September. Yards were almost crisply brown, the trees literally drooping. Yesterday, for only the second time in two months, it rained. All day. And this morning, crystalline in the sun, everything shone under a spotless sky. The air had a purity and freshness that can come only on a clear, cool fall day.

What a treat. Everything had a new look. As I pumped away, I felt the blood warming through my veins, my spirits rising to meet the promise of this exquisite morning. Choice is the word. Choice. I have been blessed with so many choice things in my life and one of the most choice is the fact that I have been fully aware of them when they occurred.

I don't know where I first learned to "relish the moment." It must have been a long, long time ago because I have had this awareness as far back as I can remember.

Well, I sure relished this morning. I even relished the relishing!

A habit that changes lives.

"The measure of mental health is the disposition to find good everywhere." I ran across this quotation from Ralph Waldo Emerson in a book by Wayne Dyer. What a world of wisdom is contained in those twelve words. I was struck not only by their insight but also by their simplicity. Think about the importance of that verb "find." It's an action word and calls for us always to be open, always aware of whatever is of a positive nature in our personal lives as well as in the world around us.

Certainly Emerson is not suggesting that our world is full of nothing but pleasing things. His point is that the habit to constantly seek for whatever tends to lift our spirits is an essential requirement for a desirable inner life.

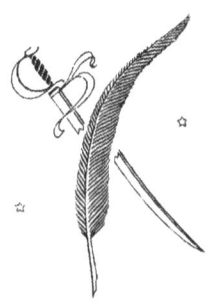

"You can't step in the same river twice."

Whoever said that gives us a starting point for understanding impermanency. This line reminds us that every experience is unique and that it will never come again in exactly the same way. What else does the river metaphor teach us? It is simply to be fully aware of whatever goodness there is in any experience we have.

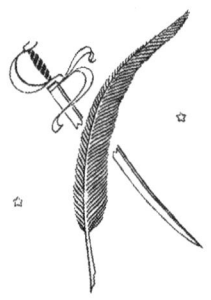

Risk.

On my walk this morning, I passed a house where a man was just coming out the front door, whistling to himself. On a whim I called to him, although he was a stranger to me, "Good morning!" I said. "You sure sound happy!" Now, I am by nature a little "reserved" you might say and didn't feel quite comfortable risking a greeting that I had no idea would be welcomed (perhaps even ignored) since the man certainly didn't know me. "Hey, hello there! It's a beautiful morning, isn't it?" he answered. "It sure is," I said. "And it's my day off!" he called. "Wonderful!" I answered.

As I walked on I felt really good about that friendly little exchange, a spontaneous expression of good will between strangers. I felt uplifted, and I think he did, too.

"Know your chief fault ...

... and commence war against it." Pretty good advice from Balthasar Gracian, the 17ᵗʰ century Spanish Jesuit. My "chief fault?" Impatience. I guess I have been "at war" against it for lo these many years. One thing in my favor, I guess, is that I realized it early in my life and became moderately successful in curbing it. It was my *awareness* of it that helped more than anything. And that is the point – the more clearly we can identify our shortcomings, the easier it is to begin to overcome them.

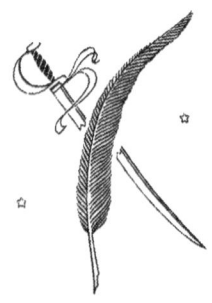

Your greatest gift to others is to be joyful.

Moods are contagious. Isn't it true that when you are around someone who is gloomy or grumpy or worrisome that before long you begin to feel the same way? A joyful, positive attitude sheds a kind of light on all who are close by and can change the tenor of a whole day for someone who may be having a bad one. It can also be a gift we can give ourselves. Even when we feel "out of sorts" or otherwise less than joyful, simply by thinking, speaking and acting positively, we can affect our own moods for the better. Psychologist William James said that "the sovereign, voluntary path to cheerfulness, if cheerfulness be lost, is to sit up cheerfully and act cheerfully, if we want cheerfulness to return."

Slippage ...

... that's a pretty good word for what has happened to many of my objectives and good intentions over the years. I create a set of goals for myself, feel enthused at having set them down in writing. And then...and then ... what happens? Well, a couple of things happen. Number one, the list is so long I shrink from starting anything. Number two, even when I prioritize there are too many things prioritized. My innate perfectionism sets in and creates a "perfect" set of ideal results that makes me breathless and tense trying to accomplish them all.

Suggestion for the future: a regular examination of progress in achieving the few most worthy goals which, when looking back ten years from now will allow me to say, "Pretty good job. Leland, overall. Not perfect, but pretty good. You can be happy with what you did with the past 10 years."

Raise your voice, lose the argument.

As soon as you show that you are angry, you give the advantage to your adversary. It just makes sense that, as wisdom suggests, "passion drives out reason" and "there's always time to add a word, never time to withdraw one." Control yourself, Leland. That way, you will always have the victory, even if it is only over yourself.

Strawberries or tigers?

There's a Zen legend about a man being chased by two tigers. He comes to the edge of a cliff, and starts to climb down, using an overhanging vine. But there at the bottom of the cliff he sees two more tigers waiting for him. He looks back up, and sees a mouse chewing through the vine he is holding onto. At that moment he sees a luscious strawberry within reach. He plucks it, and enjoys the best-tasting strawberry in his life.

So what's the message? We all have tigers in our lives, threatening our peace of mind, but we have strawberries, too – thoughts and things that make us glad. We can choose, can't we, which to focus on? I like to think we really do have a choice.

How will I feel "after?"

I woke last night with a message from somewhere. "Gauge everything with the question, 'How will you feel *after* you do or say anything?'" It seemed just another way of phrasing one of my Dad's favorite guidelines: "Live your life the way you would like to have the last chapter to turn out."

When a task or an obligation or a desire to express an opinion presents itself, asking "How will I feel 'after' I act or speak?" would provide a wonderful check on the wisdom and propriety of what I am about to do or say.

So, how to incorporate that into my daily life? Very simple. Just use this as a daily guide to setting your objectives for that day, then expand to the month, to the year, and on to the rest of your life.

Here's where you get off the track, Leland. Not reviewing often enough what you are really after: peace of mind, based on loving relationships with others and particularly with God.

It all comes down to reflecting every day on what is important for that day, as it fits into your long term goals.

Why spoil right now with "what if?"

Really, there is only *this* moment. There is simply no way possible to experience a moment that is yet to come, or to relive a moment that is past. Author Storm Jameson wrote, "There is only one minute in which you are alive: *this minute* – here and now." So why is it we so often "contaminate" (I can think of no better word) our peace of mind with that spoiler phrase, *what if*? – conjuring up unpleasant thoughts about the future? Mark Twain said that most of the "what ifs" he worried about never happened. It is a lesson hard to learn, but how wonderful, when we get the gist of it, to be fully aware of each moment, and to enjoy *right now*, uncontaminated.

The energy of love.

A French Jesuit priest once said, "Some day, after man has tamed all these energies – the tides, the winds, gravity and so forth, he will turn his mind to the energy of love. And for the second time in history man will have discovered fire."

Money worries.

Today I glanced at the TV as I passed through the room where my Patsy was watching a news program. In the lower right hand corner a red arrow pointed down with a number on it, indicating another in a series of downward dips in the Dow-Jones average. Earlier in the day, I had learned of an increase in our health insurance premium and had spent several very uptight hours on the phone trying to find out why.

I felt that old sense of unease creeping back, an unease that appears whenever an unexpected expense occurs. I have struggled with it forever, it seems. It comes in part from a depression childhood when my father was for a time unemployed and from my own forced retirement at the age of 57. But it's all so useless and unproductive.

Think of all the times I have let this happen, when all the sweat and worry didn't change a thing, yet I worked through it and today all our bills are paid and things are fine. What a waste of emotional energy, what a stupid weakness to let something like this intrude regularly on what otherwise has been a wonderful life.

Focus!

In all ways focus on what is true, beautiful, kind, loving, bright, joyous – that way you become a magnet for these kinds of things. Dwell only on the positive side of all situations and people. Don't say, "I will not talk about ..." Say rather, "I will think of only positive things," "and then *do it*."

There has been so much written about positive thinking and of its power, its magic. I do wonder how fully we realize how magical it is and what a weight negative thinking puts on our hearts and minds. I don't think we have any idea how much negativity assaults our consciousness in the space of a single week, even a single day or how often our thoughts drift into concerns about money, health, aging, the state of the world, tragedy in the news, the future. And yet not one of these types of concerns adds an iota to our sense of well-being. To worry for even one moment about something we can do nothing about is an absolute waste of that moment. Besides, I can always pray about a situation and then turn it over to God.

In the interest of love, *let it go.*

So you have been hurt by someone you love. Yes, that is hard to take. You want to retaliate in some way, either by a likewise hurtful remark or by a wounded silence. But how comforting and enabling it is to respond as Jesus would have you respond, with a silent expression of love for that person. What wonderful wisdom there is in His teaching, "to love one another." Is there anything to be gained by responding negatively? Nothing. But letting it go, in the interest of love, provides the first step towards the healing.

You better do and say what makes you like yourself because you are going to live with you 24/7 for the rest of your life.

This was a bit of self-talk that came out of nowhere on my walk this morning. It came with a kind of aggressive overtone, like a father laying out to his son the importance of a good self image that comes from making good choices. I reflected on how diminished I have felt when I have yielded to impulse and done or said something thoughtless or unwise. The sense of inner peace and self esteem that results from making the right choices is worth every effort to resist making the wrong ones.

Inexpressible.

I do not believe that anywhere on this planet has there ever been a morning more beautiful than *this* April morning. I felt myself carried to a new level of awe as I walked past trees loaded with budding leaves, flowers blooming to their fullest, the sky almost piercingly blue. It was all so inexpressibly lovely, that I am at a loss to describe it. All I could say, over and over agin, was "Thank you, God, oh I do thank you for so much beauty."

Centered.

For as long as I can remember, I have been searching for words, or concepts, or ideas which, when burned deeply and permanently into my subconscious, would shape my thoughts and behavior, always. What was needed, it seemed to me, was a *centering* on one core principle, one that would bring me the greatest sense of fulfillment when, at the end of my life, I look back and conduct my own, personal, "performance review."

After all these years I think I have discovered it. That one basic principle is ... love, God's love, which means to do the loving thing, speak the loving word, and think the loving thought, always, in all ways, and to leave all my concerns, all of them, in the loving hands of God.

No matter how much I may have protested to the contrary, my focus has been for too long on "security," on having enough money to meet our family's needs now, and in the future. Although I consider myself a Christian, too often I have failed to "let go and let God" carry my worries.

And then, there have been the stray thoughts about growing older and a momentary melancholia when I dwell too long on thinking about "the days that are no more," and "how many do I have left?"

What happens at these low points is that I have lost that priceless sense of being *centered,* of relying totally on love, God's love, as the bedrock of my life, and on my faith that God IS love, always with me through which I can receive the kind of peace of mind and joyfulness available from no other source.

How do I get it back? It's all in a shift of focus back onto love as the framework for all I do and say and, most of all, to think. As long as I hold love at the center of my life, I know I can regain that joyous peace of mind that only God can provide.

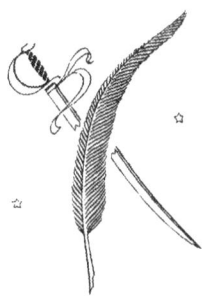

Look again.

It seems a good idea that when perceiving a negative quality in another person, we "look again" and remind ourselves that he probably struggles with self doubt and insecurity and a little loneliness, the same as you do. This idea to "look again" helps us fulfill the second great commandment, "to love our neighbor as ourselves."

The sages for centuries have been telling us this – that love, in the sense of seeing another as basically like ourselves, can help us love him, with all the weaknesses and imperfections we know to be true in our own makeup.

Love, for ourselves and for others, is our passport to our emotional health.

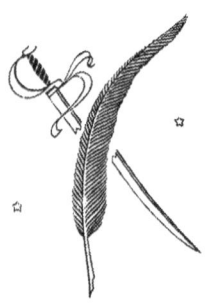

You make your own happiness.

Since ancient times we have been told that "As a man thinketh in his heart, so is he." Countless writers have repeated this basic idea in countless different ways. But the rule is the same: we create our own mental posture, our attitudes of sadness or joy by the thoughts we create and allow ourselves to dwell upon. The blind and deaf Helen Keller expressed it wonderfully: "Mine has been the limited experience of one who lives in a world without color and without sound. Yet ever since my student days, I have had the joyous certainty that my physical handicaps were not an essential part of my being since they were not a part of my mind. This truth was confirmed when I came upon Descartes' maxim, 'I think, therefore I am.' These five emphatic words waked something in me that has never slept since. I knew then that my mind could be a positive instrument of happiness, bridging over the dark, silent void, with concepts of a vibrant, light-flooded happiness. I learned that it is possible for us to create light and sound and order within us, no matter what calamity might befall us in the outer world." Anne Frank wrote similarly in her diary that she didn't think about all the ugliness in the world, but of all the beauty that still remains.

"Forgive me."

Some of us have a tough time saying we are sorry after we have said or done something unhelpful or unwise. We just don't like to admit it when we are wrong or "out of line." Our self esteem takes a little hit when we need to apologize. But it almost always brings a release from tension in a relationship gone negative. That has certainly been my experience. A sense of peace restored is certainly worth the decision to say "Forgive me."

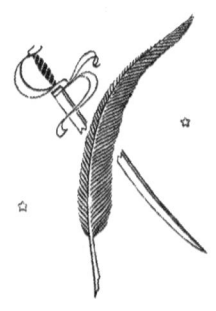

Thank you, Jesus.

I want so much to preserve the lightness and joy I felt on arising this morning (May 14, 1999). I felt the whole panorama of my life become simplified and enriched, with a quiet, newly-fresh and relaxed allegiance to Jesus. It's hard to express the feeling. Somehow, I felt lifted up, born along on a wave of quiet joy. It was a special kind of feeling, somewhat different from other times of inner happiness I have felt with an awareness of His presence. This time it was as if I was given a wondrous "second wind" for living to the fullest, and all I could respond with was, "Oh thank you, Jesus. Thank you."

I have tried to follow His teachings all my life, imperfectly and inconsistently, sometimes drifting away almost altogether. But always coming back. This time I felt the absence of struggle and stress in trying so hard to do and be what I'm supposed to do and be. I simply and quietly accepted that "amazing grace, born-again" feeling, and it was wonderful. Beyond wonderful.

Friendship.

What is this feeling I have for this group of men I meet with every Saturday morning from 7:30 to 9:00 AM? Can you think of a worse time for men to get together, regularly? Saturday morning, at 7:30 AM? It has been going on for 12 years as I write this. What do we talk about? Well, it was started by two men from our church who felt the need for a men's group to study and discuss the Bible. At first, we followed a set of published guidelines for study. Gradually, though, we found ourselves drifting from a formal curriculum to discussing more and more of the circumstances of our own lives, some trivial, some serious, but always in the spirit of a friendly concern for each other.

Our group has never grown to more than 12 or 13 at any one meeting, sometimes only five or six. But over time the same men have held the group together. Each week someone offers to lead the discussion for the following week, and someone to bring the coffee and donuts. We talk about everything from our spiritual needs (and failings) to current events, families, jobs, worries, philosophy – just about everything the leader for the day brings to the meeting.

What has grown of great value to each one of us, I feel, is something we have never discussed at all –

real friendship. I think we would feel uncomfortable discussing it. Why should it be difficult? I just don't know. Maybe it is just part of the male psyche. We have warm, affectionate regard for each other and I have no difficulty admitting it to myself, and yet I would feel uneasy expressing it to the group, or indeed to anyone individually. I am sure these feelings are reciprocated, as well as the reluctance to express them, but why should we feel uncomfortable talking about it? Not important. The friendship we feel for each other is real, and that's the main thing. The wonderful thing.

"... for beauty is God's handwriting ..."

This, from Emerson: "Never neglect an opportunity for seeing anything that is beautiful; for beauty is God's handwriting, a wayside sacrament. Welcome it in every fair face, in every fair sky and every fair flower, and thank God for it as a cup of blessing." As I walked out at sunrise on this cool October morning, the leaves burnished with sunlight, the sky a flawless blue, I thought of how many ways God makes His presence known to us. To seek the evidence that He is indeed in the world we have only to look for beauty wherever it may be. We don't have to close ourselves off in isolation, or seek Him only in church or temple. We can find Him in the colors of autumn, in heart-touching paintings, and music ... in a thousand different ways. We find the blessed assurance that God is around us whenever and wherever we experience beauty.

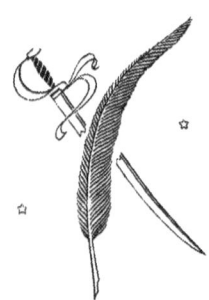

Quotations Worth Remembering, and Reviewing, Often.

(Note: For over 60 years, I have been a collector of a wide variety of quotations providing insight and wisdom. Occasionally, however, I carelessly neglected to note sources. In preparing this book I have spent countless hours attempting to locate origins of some of the quotations cited. My sincere apologies to the authors, and to readers, for having to use the term "Anon" occasionally in the absence of credit.)

**I simply believe that some part of the human SELF is not subject to the laws of time and space.
– Carl Gustaf Jung**

Prayer is indeed good, but while calling on the Gods a man should himself lend a hand. – Hippocrates

Most people live, whether physically, intellectually, or morally, in the very restricted circle of their potential being. They make use of a very small portion of their possible consciousness, and of their soul's resources in general, much like a man, who, out of his whole bodily organism, should get into the habit of using and moving only his little finger. Great emergencies and crises show us how much greater our vital resources are than we had supposed.
– William James

We little know how near to despair our neighbor may be even though he mask it with smiles. – Nora Holm

Pure religion is love in action. – Anon

Follow your bliss. – Joseph Campbell

God loves an idle rainbow no less than
the laboring seas. – Anon

Love more, demand less. – Anon

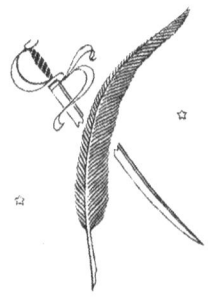

He drew a circle that shut me out.
Heretic, rebel, a thing to flout.
But love and I had the wit to win;
We drew a circle that took him in.
– Edwin Markham

What is the part of wisdom? To dream, with one eye open; to be detached from the world without being hostile to it; to welcome fugitive beauties and pity fugitive sufferings, never forgetting for one moment how fugitive they are.
– George Santayana

There is always time to add a word, never time to withdraw one. – Anon

Two men looked out from behind prison bars. One saw the mud, and the other the stars. – Anon

Those who know the truth are not equal to those who love it. – Anon

Time and reflection have a wonderful way of weeding out the trivial.
– Leland Davis

The best things in life are not things.
– Anon

... the historian records the exceptional because it is interesting - because it is exceptional ... Behind the red façade of war and politics, misfortune and poverty, adultery and divorce, murder and suicide, were millions of orderly homes, devoted marriages, men and women kindly and affectionate, troubled and happy with children. Even in recorded history, we find so many instances of goodness, even of nobility, that we can forgive, though not forget, the sins. Who will dare to write a history of human goodness?
– Will and Ariel Durant

The positive emotions can block the panic and the depression and the despair that all too often figure in the onset of disease or the intensification of disease ... A lot of us are starved for joy, and yet there's a lot of it out there. It's not going to happen automatically but it's worth working for. You have to work at making joy. – Norman Cousins

Our life is frittered away by detail. Simplify! Simplify!
– Henry David Thoreau

There is perhaps no greater mark of folly than to attempt to correct the natural infirmities of those we love.
– Henry Fielding

A man is rich in proportion to the things he can afford to let alone.
– Henry David Thoreau

What religion a man shall have is a historical accident, quite as much as what language he shall speak.
– George Santayana

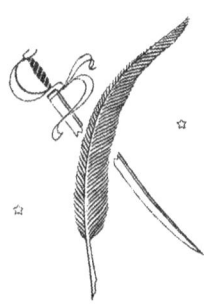

My theology, briefly, is that the universe was dictated but not signed.
– Christopher Morley

To understand another human being you must gain some insight into the conditions which made him what he is. – Margaret Bourke-White

Besides the noble art of getting things done, there is the noble art of leaving things undone. The wisdom of life consists in the elimination of non-essentials. – Lin Yutang

I think it is very important to stay interested, to stay vitally interested in world affairs; to have some religious interest is very important; to have interest in other people; to have a community of people with whom you really share things, not superficially, but with whom you share your worries as well as your triumphs. I see the possibility of having a very good old age. – George Leonard

To do nothing is sometimes a good remedy. – Hippocrates

Carpe diem, quam minimus credula postero. Seize the day and put as little trust as you can in tomorrow.
– Horace

Of all the systems of morality, ancient or modern, that have come unto my observation, none appears to me so pure as that of Jesus. – Thomas Jefferson

I know! I have had the experience of been gripped by something stronger than myself, something that people call God. – Carl Gustaf Jung

Remember this, that very little is needed to make a happy life.
– Marcus Aurelius

Ancora imparo. I am still learning.
– Michelangelo

It is the heart that experiences God, and not reason. This, then, is faith: God felt by the heart, not reason.
– Blaise Pascal

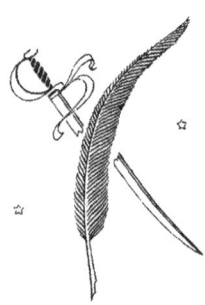

The heart has reasons which reason does not understand. – Anon

It takes a very long time to become young. – Pablo Picasso

There is a major difference between denying real problems and the avoidance or agonizing over those things we cannot change. Denial is dangerous, for it results from failure to acknowledge facts. Avoidance is healthy, because avoidance is the dismissal from our lives of those implications and speculations about which we can do nothing. When we understand that every thought we have results in a spurt of psychochemicals, we begin to realize the power we have not only to destroy ourselves but to enjoy ourselves. – Paul Pearsall

I do not feel obliged to believe that the same God who has endowed us with sense, reason, and intellect has intended us to forego their use. – Galileo

It is the sense of mystery that, in my opinion, drives the true scientist ... that drives the larva into the butterfly. If [the scientist] has not experienced, at least a few times in his life, this cold shudder down his spine, this confrontation with an immense invisible face whose breath moves him to tears, he is not a scientist. – Edwin Chargaff, biologist

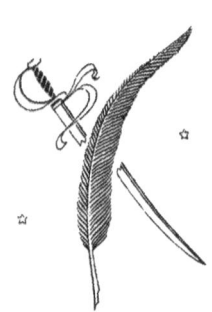

The important thing is not to stop questioning. Curiosity has its own reason for existing. One cannot help but be in awe when he contemplates the mystery of eternity, of life, of the marvelous structure of reality. It is enough if one tries to comprehend a little of this mystery every day.
– Albert Einstein

Once we see, however, that the probability of life originating at random is so utterly minuscule as to make it absurd, it becomes sensible to think that the favorable properties of physics on which life depends are in every respect deliberate ... It is therefore almost inevitable that our own measure of intelligence must reflect ... higher intelligences ... even to the limit of God ... – Sir Fred Hoyle, British mathematician, astronomer and cosmologist

Be like a bird who pausing in her flight, on boughs too slight, feels them give way beneath her and yet sings, knowing that she has wings. – Anon

The forms and creeds of religions change, but the sentiment of religion – the wonder and reverence and love we feel in the presence of the inscrutable universe we feel – persists.
– John Burroughs

There is for me powerful evidence that there is something going on behind it all ... It seems that somebody has fine-tuned nature's numbers to make the Universe . . . The impression of design is overwhelming. – Paul Davies

Science conducts us, step by step, through the whole range of creation, until we arrive, at length, at God.
– Marguerite De Valois

The human mind is not capable of grasping the Universe. We are like a little child entering a huge library. The walls are covered to the ceilings in many different tongues. The child knows that someone must have written these books. It does not know who or how. It does not understand the languages in which they are written. But the child notes a definite plan in the arrangement of the books . . . a mysterious order which it does not comprehend, but only dimly suspects. – Albert Einstein

Who spread it's canopy?
Or its curtains spun?
Who in this bowling alley
bowled the sun?
– Edward Taylor

The day will come when, after harnessing space, the winds, the tides, and gravitation, we shall harness for God the energies of love. And on that day, for the second time in the history of the world, we shall have discovered fire. – Pierre Teilhard Chardin

Silence is a friend who will never betray. – Anon

The world is my country, all mankind are my brethren, and to do good is my religion. – Thomas Paine

The difference between religions is the difference in their relative content of agnosticism. The most satisfying and ecstatic faith is almost purely agnostic. It trusts absolutely without professing to know at all. – H. L. Mencken

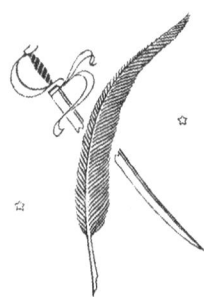

There is no such thing in anyone's life as an unimportant day.
– Alexander Woolcott

Our emotions don't happen to us so much as we choose them. In fact, our own thoughts, emotions, and actions are the only things we really do control. In the first century A.D., the Greek thinker Epictetus made this fact the foundation of his philosophy, declaring that all unhappiness arises from attempts to control events and other people over which one has no power. The same futile attempt born of our fears and resentments, weakens the body and tends to disease.
– Bernie Siegel, M.D.

It is part of the cure to wish to be cured.
– Lucious Annaeus Seneca

It is the grossest of mistakes to assume that the limit of our power of perception is also the limit to all there is to perceive.
– Anon

If the work of God could be comprehended by reason, it would be no longer wonderful, and faith would have no merit if reason provided proof. – St. Gregory I

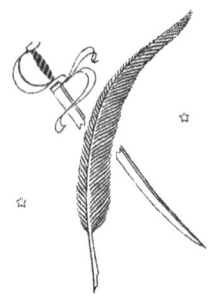

The heart of the matter is a very simple and old-fashioned thing, a thing so simple that I am almost ashamed to mention it, for fear of the derisive smile with which wise cynics will greet my words. The thing I mean - please forgive me for mentioning it - is love, Christian love, or compassion. – Bertrand Russell

I find it quite improbable that such order came out of chaos. There has to be some organizing principle. God to me is a mystery but is the explanation for the miracle of existence, why there is something instead of nothing.
– Alan Sandage, astronomer

A common sense interpretation of the facts suggests that a super intellect has monkeyed with physics, as well as with chemistry and biology, and that there are no blind forces worth speaking about in nature. The numbers one calculates from the facts seem to me so overwhelming as to put this conclusion almost beyond question.
– Sir Fred Hoyle, British mathematician, astronomer and cosmologist

With all your science can you tell, how it is, and whence it is, that light comes into the soul? – Henry David Thoreau

There are more things, in heaven and Earth, Horatio, than are dreamt of in your philosophy.
– William Shakespeare

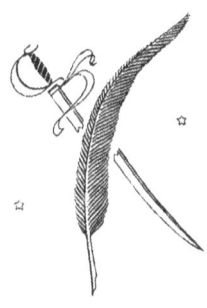

Scripture and Prayers Worth Remembering and Reviewing, Often

If any man be in Christ, he is a new creature: old things are passed away; behold, all things are become new.
(II Corinthians 5:17)

Fear thou not for I am with thee: be not dismayed, for I am thy God: I will strengthen thee; I will help thee; yea, I will uphold thee with the right hand of my righteousness. (Isaiah 41:10)

Thy sun shall no more go down; neither shall thy moon withdraw itself: for the Lord shall be thine everlasting light, and the days of thy mourning shall be ended. (Isaiah 60:20)

Finally, Brethren, whatsoever things are true, whatsoever things are honest, whatsoever things are just, whatsoever things are pure, whatsoever things are lovely, whatsoever things are of good report; if there be any virtue, and if there be any praise, think on these things. (Philippians 4:8)

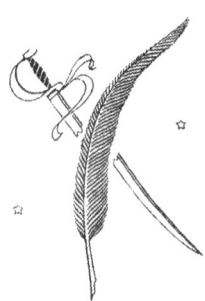

The Lord is near, have no anxiety, but in everything make your requests be known to God in prayer and petition with thanksgiving. Then the peace of God, which is beyond our utmost understanding, will keep guard over your hearts and your thoughts, in Christ Jesus. (Philippians 4: 6, 7)

In all thy ways acknowledge him, and he shall direct thy paths.   (Proverbs 3:6)

And thine ears shall hear a word behind thee, saying, This is the way, walk ye in it, when ye turn to the right hand, and when ye turn to the left.
(Isaiah 30:21)

But they that wait upon the Lord shall renew their strength; they shall mount up with wings of eagles; they shall run, and not be weary; and they shall walk, and not faint. (Isaiah 40:31)

He hath showed thee, oh man, what is good; and what doth the Lord require of thee, but to do justly, and to love mercy, and to walk humbly with thy God? (Micah 6:8)

For I am persuaded that neither death, nor life, nor angels, nor principalities, nor powers, nor things present, nor things to come, nor height, nor depth, nor any other creature shall be able to separate us from the love of God, which is in Christ Jesus, our Lord.
(Romans 8: 38, 39)

For thou hast been a strength to the poor, a strength to the needy in his distress, a refuge from the storm, a shadow from the heat, when the blast from the terrible ones is as a storm against the wall. (Isaiah 25:4)

Come, my people, enter into thy chambers, and shut thy doors about thee; hide thyself as it were for a little moment until the indignation be overpast. (Isaiah 26:20)

In quietness and confidence shall be your strength. (Isaiah 30:15)

He that dwelleth in the secret place of the most High shall abide under the shadow of the Almighty. I will say of the Lord, He is my refuge and my fortress; my God; in him will I trust.
(Psalms 91:1, 2)

I have blotted out, as a thick cloud ... thy sins: return unto me; for I have redeemed thee. (Isaiah 44:22)

Be strong and of good courage; be not afraid, neither be thou dismayed: for the Lord thy God is with thee, whithersoever thou goest.
(Joshua 1:9)

The Lord will perfect that which concerneth me. (Psalms 138:8)

... and, lo, I am with you alway, even unto the end of the world.
(Matthew 28:20)

I sought the Lord, and he heard me, and delivered me from all my fears.
(Psalms 34:4)

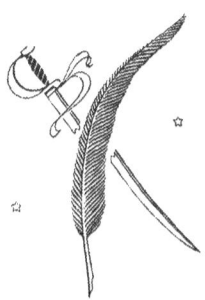

... but to be spiritually minded is life and peace. (Romans 8:6)

For the law of the spirit of life in Christ Jesus hath made me free from the law of sin and death. (Romans 8:2)

Be still, and know that I am God. (Psalms 46:10)

Thou wilt keep him in perfect peace whose mind is stayed on thee. (Isaiah 26:3)

In nothing be anxious; but in everything by prayer and supplications with thanksgiving let your requests be made known to God. (Philippians 4:6)

The Lord is my light and my salvation; whom shall I fear? The Lord is the strenght of my life; of whom shall I be afraid? (Psalms 27:1)

Cast thy burden on the Lord, and he shall sustain thee. (Psalms 55:22)

In the Lord put I my trust: how say ye unto my soul, flee as a bird to your mountain? (Psalms 11:1)

For God hath not given us a spirit of fear; but of power and of love and of a sound mind. (II Timothy 1:7)

The light of God surrounds me; the love of God enfolds me; the power of God protects me; the presence of God watches over me. Wherever I am, God is. – St. Teresa of Avila

Let my soul find refuge from the crowding turmoil of worldly thoughts beneath the shadow of thy wings. Let my heart, this sea of restless waves, find peace in thee, oh God. – Anon

Let nothing disturb thee; let nothing dismay thee; all things pass; God never changes. Patience attains all that it strives for. He who has God finds he lacks nothing; God alone suffices.
– St. Teresa of Avila

I have blotted out, as a thick cloud and, as a cloud, thy sins: return unto me; for I have redeemed thee. (Isaiah 44:22)

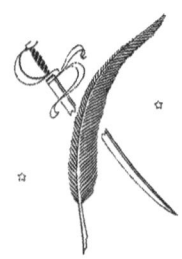

The Lord is my shepherd;
I shall not want.
He maketh me to lie down
in green pastures; he leadeth me
beside the still waters.
He restoreth my soul: he
leadeth me in the paths of
righteousness for his name sake.
Yea, though I walk through
the valley of the shadow of
death, I will fear no evil: for
thou art with me; thy rod and
thy staff they comfort me.
Thou preparest a table
before me in the presence of
mine enemies; thou anointest
my head with oil; my cup
runneth over.
Surely goodness and mercy
shall follow me all the days of
my life: and I will dwell in the
house of the Lord forever.
(Psalms 23)